D0745583

DISCARD

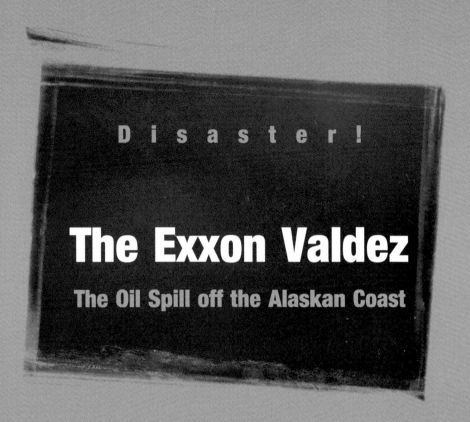

Disaster!

The Exxon Valdez

The Oil Spill off the Alaskan Coast

by Tom Streissguth

002000259047

CAPSTONE
HIGH-INTEREST
BOOKS

an imprint of Capstone Press
Mankato, Minnesota

Farmington Public Library
2101 Farmington Avenue
Farmington, N.M. 87401

Capstone High-Interest Books are published by Capstone Press
151 Good Counsel Drive, P.O. Box 669, Mankato, Minnesota 56002
http://www.capstone-press.com

Copyright © 2003 by Capstone Press. All rights reserved.
No part of this publication may be reproduced in whole or in part, or stored in a retrieval system, or transmitted in any form or by any means, electronic, mechanical, photocopying, recording, or otherwise, without written permission of the publisher. For information regarding permission, write to Capstone Press,
151 Good Counsel Drive, P.O. Box 669, Dept. R, Mankato, Minnesota 56002
Printed in the United States of America.

Library of Congress Cataloging-in-Publication Data
Streissguth, Thomas, 1958–
    The Exxon Valdez: the oil spill off the Alaskan Coast/by Tom Streissguth.
    p. cm.—(Disaster!)
    Summary: Describes the oil tanker Exxon Valdez, the events that led up to its disastrous oil spill in 1989, and the effects of the spill on the Alaskan environment.
    Includes bibliographical references and index.
    ISBN 0-7368-1320-9 (hardcover)
    1. Oil spills—Environmental aspects—Alaska—Prince William Sound Region—Juvenile literature. 2. Tankers—Accidents—Environmental aspects—Alaska—Prince William Sound Region—Juvenile literature. 3. Exxon Valdez (Ship)—Juvenile literature. [1. Oil spills—Alaska—Prince William Sound region. 2. Tankers—Accidents. 3. Exxon Valdez (Ship).] I. Title. II. Disaster! (Capstone High-Interest Books)
TD427.P4 S77 2003
363.738'2'097983—dc21   2001008336

Editorial Credits

Matt Doeden, editor; Karen Risch, product planning editor; Kia Adams,
    book designer and illustrator; Jo Miller, photo researcher

Photo Credits

AFP/CORBIS, 9
AP/Wide World Photos/John Gaps III, cover
Bettmann/CORBIS, 6, 26–27
Charles Mason/Black Star/Timepix, 21
Hulton Archive by Getty Images, 16
McVay/Folio, Inc., 19
PhotoDisc, Inc., 8
Roy Corral/CORBIS, 12–13
U.S. Coast Guard Photo, 4, 10, 22

Special thanks to the Environmental Protection Agency's Region 10 office for their help in preparing this book.

1 2 3 4 5 6 07 06 05 04 03 02

Table of Contents

Features

Fast Facts about the *Exxon Valdez*

Length: 987 feet (301 meters)

Weight: 212,000 tons
(192,326 metric tons)

Cost: $125 million

Date of Spill: March 24, 1989

Amount of Spill: 267,000 barrels
(11 million gallons; 42 million liters)

Cost of Cleanup: $2.2 billion

Death Toll Estimates: 250,000
seabirds; 2,800 sea otters;
300 harbor seals; 250 bald eagles;
22 killer whales; 400 loons; and
countless fish

Current Name: *SeaRiver Mediterranean*

CHAPTER ONE

The Disaster

On March 23, 1989, ships,
ferries, and tugboats crowded
the harbor of Valdez, Alaska.
One of the large ships was the
Exxon Valdez. This tanker
carried 53 million gallons
(200 million liters) of crude oil.

The *Exxon Valdez* slowly
pulled out of the harbor.
The ship's captain, Joseph
Hazelwood, set a course
for Prince William Sound.
This area stretches along the
southwestern coast of Alaska.
From there, the ship would
take the oil to California.

Running Aground

Just before midnight, Hazelwood left the ship's bridge for the night. He left an officer named Gregory Cousins in command of the ship.

Workers pumped oil from the *Exxon Valdez* into a second tanker after the spill.

Hazelwood told Cousins to steer the ship around Bligh Reef ahead. Hazelwood knew that the reef's sharp rocks and shallow areas were dangerous to a large ship.

Cousins took over command, but he did not follow Hazelwood's orders. Instead, Cousins went into the chart room to study maps of Prince William Sound. The ship continued on a straight course toward Bligh Reef.

Four minutes after midnight on March 24, the *Exxon Valdez* passed directly over the reef. The sharp rocks ripped several holes in the bottom of the ship's hull. The rocks tore open tanks holding the ship's crude oil. The oil gushed into the water.

The collision shook the entire ship. Hazelwood rushed back to the bridge. He ordered his officers to move the ship slowly forward. But the *Exxon Valdez* could not move. It was stuck on Bligh Reef.

Crude Oil

Oil companies drill deep inside the Earth for crude oil. This thick, black substance is created over millions of years from decaying plant and animal matter. Oil companies use large factories called refineries to make crude oil into fuels such as gasoline and natural gas.

The Spill

Oil quickly spread in the water around the *Exxon Valdez*. By morning, a huge black pool surrounded the tanker. The wind and tides pushed the oil toward shore. Everything in sight was covered in a thin black layer of oil.

Experts quickly realized what a disaster the oil spill was. The U.S. Coast Guard worked with the Alaska Department of Environmental Conservation and other groups to decide how to handle the spill. They could not stop the oil from leaking out of the ship. Instead, they began pumping the remaining oil out of the tanks.

Crews worked day and night to pump oil left in the *Exxon Valdez* into another tanker. This job was dangerous. Strong winds caused rough waters. The oil still floated all around the ship. A single spark could have caused a huge explosion.

On April 4, the ship's tanks were finally empty. The next day, crews pushed the ship off Bligh Reef and helped it return to Valdez. The mess it left behind was the worst oil spill in U.S. history.

Tugboats pulled the *Exxon Valdez* off Bligh Reef.

CHAPTER TWO

History and Design

Exxon is one of the world's biggest oil companies. It uses large ships called oil tankers to carry crude oil to places all over the world. Valdez, Alaska, is one of Exxon's most important harbors. Most of the oil pumped in Alaska goes to Valdez through the Trans-Alaska Pipeline. Oil tankers carry much of this oil to refineries along North America's West Coast.

Ship Design

The *Exxon Valdez* was launched in 1986. It was the first model of a new kind of ship called an Alaska-class tanker. At the time, the *Exxon Valdez* was the largest ship ever built on the West Coast of the United States. It cost about $125 million to build.

The *Exxon Valdez* was the most modern oil tanker in Exxon's fleet. The ship could hold as much as 1.48 million barrels of oil. Its job was to carry the oil from Alaska to the West Coast of the United States.

Eleven tanks held the oil inside the ship. The *Exxon Valdez* also had four ballast tanks. The ballast tanks held water. Officers could change the water levels inside the ballast tanks to adjust the ship's weight.

The *Exxon Valdez*'s superstructure was at the

rear of the ship. The superstructure rose above the rest of the ship. It included the bridge, crew quarters, the kitchens, and the chart rooms. The engine room was at the back of the ship. It housed a single diesel engine that could push the ship to a speed of about 19 miles (31 kilometers) per hour.

The *Exxon Valdez* was the first model of the Alaska-class tanker.

Damage to the Ship

The *Exxon Valdez*'s hull was made of welded steel. Some tanker ships have double hulls to prevent spills, but the *Exxon Valdez* had only a single hull.

The collision with Bligh Reef ripped open the *Exxon Valdez*'s single hull in several places. The worst damage was to the ship's front. The sharp rocks tore through the underside of the ship. Oil immediately began to leak from the holes.

The rocks continued to tear open a wide gash along the underside of the hull until the

Layout of the *Exxon Valdez*

		Slop Tank	#5 Cargo Tank	#4 Ballast Tank	
Engine Room		#5 Cargo Tank Center		#4 Cargo Tank Center	
		Slop Tank	#5 Cargo Tank	#4 Ballast Tank	

ship came to a stop. The forward tank was badly damaged. Four of the central tanks also were completely torn open. A fifth central tank was slightly damaged. One of the ballast tanks was also destroyed. The tanks at the rear of the ship suffered only light damage.

Most of the oil spilled out of the ship within the first eight hours. The badly damaged tanks spilled very quickly. About 115,000 barrels of oil escaped from these tanks within 30 minutes of the collision. This amount was nearly half of the total spill. The oil spilled more slowly from the tanks that had minor damage.

Port Side

#3 Cargo Tank	#2 Ballast Tank	#1 Cargo Tank
#3 Cargo Tank Center	#2 Cargo Tank Center	#1 Cargo Tank Center
#3 Cargo Tank	#2 Ballast Tank	#1 Cargo Tank

Starboard Side

Learn About:

- Cleanup efforts
- The investigation
- Trials and punishments

After the Spill

The *Exxon Valdez* disaster did not end when the ship left Prince William Sound. A layer of oil spread for hundreds of miles. Thousands of fish died under the oil. Birds died when the oil covered their wings.

The oil quickly washed to shore. It covered rocks, sand, plants, and any other objects it touched. It even moved into streams. Mammals such as sea otters, sea lions, and whales were covered in oil. Most of these animals died.

Cleaning Up

Thousands of people helped clean the mess left by the oil spill. Experts tried many methods to remove oil from the water. People scrubbed oil from rocks along the coast. Others used hoses to spray oil from beaches. The Environmental Protection Agency (EPA) even used special bacteria in the cleanup effort. These microscopic creatures ate the oil that stuck to some beaches.

Many people worried about the injured animals. People cleaned birds and otters that had been covered in oil. They saved some of the animals, but many of the rescued animals could no longer live on their own. Some were sent to zoos. There, they received continuing medical care.

Most animals could not be rescued. More than 250,000 birds died. Hundreds of seals, whales, and otters also died. Other animals lost their ability to produce young. The damage from the spill still affects many animal populations today.

Workers tried to clean the oil that stuck
to hundreds of miles of coastline.

The Blame for the Spill

People were angry with Exxon for all the damage and suffering the spill caused. The U.S. government investigated the accident.

Investigators studied the damage to the ship. They spoke to Hazelwood, Cousins, and other crew members. The investigators learned that Cousins had not followed Hazelwood's order to steer the ship around Bligh Reef. But Cousins was only partly to blame. Hazelwood also had made a serious mistake. Company rules stated that two officers must be on the bridge at all times. Hazelwood had left Cousins alone.

Hazelwood made another mistake. He was drinking alcohol the night of the spill. Investigators wondered if Hazelwood's drinking could have affected his judgment.

Trials

The U.S. government and the state of Alaska sued Exxon for the accident. A judge ordered Exxon to pay more than $5 billion for the damage. Exxon also had to pay for the cleanup.

Hazelwood went on trial in Anchorage, Alaska. The jury found him guilty of dumping oil into Prince William Sound. The court sentenced him to 1,000 hours of community service. He was supposed to clean the beaches that the spill had ruined. But Hazelwood appealed his sentence. He asked a different court to lift the sentence. His appeal failed, but it took so long that the cleanup efforts already had ended. In 1999, Hazelwood had to pick up trash from roads near Anchorage instead.

An Alaskan court sentenced Joseph Hazelwood to 1,000 hours of community service for his role in the spill.

What We Have Learned

Today, the waters of Prince William Sound are mostly clean. Storms have helped to clean much of the coastline. But oil from the *Exxon Valdez* accident still remains in some areas. Oil beneath rocks has dried and hardened. This oil may remain for many years.

Recovery

Thousands of people worked to save the wildlife that the oil spill affected. Cleanup efforts kept going even months after the spill. The efforts helped lessen the damage in some places, but repairing all of the damage will take a long time. Fish that live in streams along Prince William Sound still suffer from the effects of the oil. Their populations have not recovered since the spill.

Scientists have studied the area's wildlife since the spill. They have learned that some animals recover more quickly than others. Populations of bald eagles, killer whales, and salmon have already recovered. Seal and sea otter populations have not recovered. These animals were once very common along Prince William Sound. Today, their populations are much smaller.

The spill also affected the people of Alaska. Many Alaskans rely on fishing to earn a living. Some native people have relied on fishing for thousands of years. The spill badly damaged the fishing industry. It still has not fully recovered.

Tourism is another important industry in Alaska. People take trips there to enjoy the scenery. The spill drove away many tourists. The people of Alaska lost millions of dollars from the loss of these tourists.

Spread of Oil from *Exxon Valdez*

ALASKA

• Anchorage

• Valdez

Prince William Sound

N
W
E
S

ALASKA

CANADA

Map Legend

Spread of Oil

Changes

The *Exxon Valdez* disaster changed the way ships move in and out of Valdez. The U.S. Coast Guard now keeps a 24-hour watch on all traffic in the harbor. Tugboats, rescue craft, and boats designed to clean oil spills are ready at all times.

After the spill, Exxon changed the name of the *Exxon Valdez* to *Exxon Mediterranean*.

Many organizations worked to clean up the *Exxon Valdez* spill, but they often did not communicate with one another. The disaster helped cleanup crews learn to work together. Experts hope that cleanup efforts of future oil spills will be better organized.

In 1990, the U.S. Congress passed the Oil Pollution Act. This new law required all future oil tankers to have a double hull. Lawmakers hope this extra protection will prevent such large spills in the future. But some oil companies are fighting this law. They say that ships with double hulls are too expensive to build.

Exxon spent about $25 million to repair the damage to the *Exxon Valdez*. Company officials then renamed the ship *Exxon Mediterranean*. Later, the ship's name was changed to *SeaRiver Mediterranean*. Today, it carries oil between the Middle East and Europe. Alaskan lawmakers passed a law preventing the ship from ever working near Alaska again.

Timeline

Oil is discovered in the North Slope region of Alaska.

The *Exxon Valdez* begins operation as an oil tanker; the ship carries crude oil from the port of Valdez, Alaska, to the West Coast of the United States.

1968   **1977**   **1986**   **1989**

Work is completed on the Trans-Alaska Pipeline; crude oil travels about 800 miles (1,287 kilometers) from the North Slope to the port of Valdez.

March 23—The *Exxon Valdez* leaves the port of Valdez, Alaska, on a routine trip.

March 27—Strong winds drive the oil along hundreds of miles of Alaskan coastline.

March 24—Four minutes after midnight, the *Exxon Valdez* strikes Bligh Reef in Prince William Sound; the collision spills oil into the water.

The U.S. Congress passes the Oil Pollution Act.

1989   **1989**   **1990**   **1999**

April 5—The *Exxon Valdez* is pushed off Bligh Reef and returns to Valdez, Alaska, for repairs.

Captain Joseph Hazelwood begins serving 1,000 hours of community service as his punishment for the oil spill.

Words to Know

ballast (BAL-uhst)—heavy material, such as water, carried in a ship to make it more stable

bridge (BRIJ)—the control center of a ship; crew members steered the *Exxon Valdez* from this room.

crude oil (KROOD OIL)—a thick, black substance drilled from the Earth and used to make fuels such as gasoline and natural gas

harbor (HAR-bur)—an area where ships load and unload cargo

hull (HUHL)—the main body of a ship or boat

reef (REEF)—a strip of rock, coral, or sand near the surface of the ocean

superstructure (SOO-pur-struhk-chur)—the part of a ship that rises above the main deck

tanker (TANG-kur)—a large ship designed to carry liquids such as crude oil

To Learn More

Dils, Tracey E. *The Exxon Valdez.* Great Disasters, Reforms and Ramifications. Philadelphia: Chelsea House, 2001.

Sandler, Martin. *America's Great Disasters.* New York: HarperCollins, 2002.

Sherrow, Victoria. *The Exxon Valdez: Tragic Oil Spill.* American Disasters. Springfield, N.J.: Enslow, 1998.

Useful Addresses

Environmental Protection Agency
Region 10 Headquarters
1200 Sixth Avenue
Seattle, WA 98101

United States Coast Guard Headquarters
2100 Second Street SW
Washington, DC 20593-0001

Internet Sites

Anchorage Daily News—Legacy of the Exxon Valdez Oil Spill
http://www.adn.com/evos/evos.html

EPA—Exxon Valdez
http://www.epa.gov/oilspill/exxon.htm

Exxon Valdez Oil Spill
http://library.thinkquest.org/10867/intro/index.shtml

Index